HAIKU HUMOR

HAIKU
HUMOR

By Stephen Addiss

with Fumiko
and Akira Yamamoto

BOSTON   WEATHERHILL   LONDON

2007

Weatherhill
an imprint of
Shambhala Publications, Inc.
Horticultural Hall
300 Massachusetts Avenue
Boston, Massachusetts 02115
www.shambhala.com

9 8 7 6 5 4 3 2 1

First Edition
Printed in China

♾This edition is printed on acid-free paper
that meets the American National Standards
Institute Z39.48 Standard.

Distributed in the United States by Random House, Inc.,
and in Canada by Random House of Canada Ltd

Library of Congress Cataloging-in-Publication Data

Addiss, Stephen, 1935–
Haiku humor / by Stephen Addiss with Fumiko
and Akira Yamamoto.
p.   cm.
Includes bibliographical references and index.
ISBN 978-1-59030-472-3 (alk. paper)
1. Haiku—History and criticism. 2. Humor in
literature.
I. Yamamoto, Fumiko. II. Yamamoto, Akira. III. Title.
PL729.A35 2007
895.6′1041—dc22
2007009216

CONTENTS

Dedicated to Yoshiko
for her appreciation of humor

Introduction

Humor has long been a lively element in Japanese cultural tradition; during the past four centuries, it has taken an increasingly important role. From the complete reunification of Japan in 1615, after a century of civil wars, and in the strong grip of often repressive governments, until the collapse of the Tokugawa Shogunate in 1868, the country was deliberately cut off from the rest of the world. People were firmly set into a closed class structure; one's profession was mostly determined by heredity, and even entertainment, clothing, and travel were strictly regulated. Although there were times of peace and relative prosperity, for most common people, their life course ran fairly much on socially and politically laid down tracks.

During these centuries of a stratified and controlled society, humor became a means to cope. Faced with the discord between the ways a society is expected to work and the actual world of human behavior and awareness of environment, acceptance of life's tension through humor was uplifting and life affirming. Japanese humor took many forms including parody, satire, absurdist humor, fantasy, sexual humor, puns, gender humor, wit, caricature, and visual humor. Among them, haiku, which bloomed into its full glory during the Edo period (1603–1867), became one of the vehicles for expressing literary playfulness.

Haiku, originally called *haikai* (comical verse), evolved from the first three lines of elegant *waka* poetry of 5-7-5-7-7 syllables, and from the beginning was imbued with a sense of lightheartedness. In the poetic game of linked verse (*renga*), a popular pastime from about the thirteenth century to the early Edo period, poets composed a string of waka poetry in which one poet's 5-7-5 syllables was followed by another poet's addition of 7-7 syllables. *Renga* is full of intricate mood turns, showing off each contributor's poetic skill and wit, bringing in a new light or often a twist to the flow of the verses, while keeping attuned to the main theme. From this practice of linked verse, haiku (haikai) took its stance, reflecting poets' delight in esprit. Matsuo Bashō (1644–1694), the most famous haiku poet, was a skilled player of this poetic composition game.

If there is a single feature that constantly recurs in haiku humor, it is an element of surprise, a new discovery in common phenomena. A surprise is only possible when there is first a normative pattern that can be violated. A pattern is necessary because it causes us to form certain expectations, and when these expectations are not met, amusement emerges. The Japanese feudal political system firmly planted what was expected in the societal milieu, while the long tradition of literary genre, especially waka, had cultivated people's acceptance of what poetic beauty should be. The surprise caused by breaking established formulae, either social or literary, served as the source for haiku humor.

A wonderful example is the following haiku from the celebrated poet, Kobayashi Issa (1762–1826). Here he muses at his brazier (*kotatsu*) at a scene parading in front of his house:

> Soaked in the rain
> a *daimyō* is passing
> by my warm kotatsu

Commoners had to kneel down by the roadside when they

encountered a daimyō's procession. Yet Issa is enjoying himself at his toasty foot-warmer in the haven of his house while a warlord's procession is struggling through the hard-driven winter rain. It is this subtle and playful shift in our perception that makes haiku humor distinctive. While Issa's social station is humble, his joy in life, like that of many haiku poets, comes from his commoner's status. At the base of haiku humor lies a sense of balance—nothing is too large, too small, or too extreme. Looking at Issa again, we can see that he also knows his limitations:

> The auspiciousness
> is just about medium—
> my spring

The smiles derived from haiku are usually benign and gentle, often leading to the reader's empathy with a discovery of something new in the ordinary. This may be brought out by an unanticipated contrast:

> After my sneeze
> all is quiet—
> summer mountains
> *Yasui*

The sound created by one humble human vibrates through the whole area, and the poet is impressed by the effect of his own action and how it enhances the silence around him.

Empathy can arise from a close-up description of something that people do not usually notice:

> After a short night—
> on the hairy caterpillar
> pearls of dew
> *Buson*

Here the poet's eyes are focused on a tiny creature, admiring its unusual ornaments.

Exaggeration is another form of humor, for example, where the poet miniaturizes himself as an observer:

> Opening the red gate
> of the Ant King's Palace—
> a peony
>
> *Buson*

The hardworking black foot soldiers tirelessly go in and out of a gorgeous gate for their royalty. It is a lively microcosm, inviting the readers to fantasy.

Personification is also very much favored by haiku poets as a source of wry humor.

> Sad stories
> whispered to the jellyfish
> by the sea slug
>
> *Shōha*

Issa was the greatest master of the art of personification. In his haiku, any living being can become our companion.

> Opening his mouth to say
> "this day is much too long"—
> a crow

> Don't hit me!
> the fly wrings its hands
> and wrings its feet

Indeed, for Issa every creature is equal in this world:

> When there are people
> there are flies, and also
> there are Buddhas

Many haiku bring warmhearted smiles, yet poets also recognize that this world is transitory. Their observation of life sometimes reflects sympathy mixed with a touch of resignation:

> Here we are
> all skeletons—
> evening cool
>
> *Issa*

> Our skeletons
> dressing up in finery—
> flower viewing
> *Onitsura*

Poets are keenly aware of the impermanence of life, but because of it, they cherish and sing of the precious moment of joy.

> Under the trees
> into the salad, into the soup—
> cherry blossoms
> *Bashō*

Haiku humor is gentle, while the laughter caused by human folly is the specialty of haiku's mocking and farcical twin, *senryū,* which became enormously popular about two hundred years later than haiku. Like haiku, senryū developed its 5-7-5 format from the first part of classical waka poems of 5-7-5-7-7 syllables. Many old senryū do not include authors' names, reflecting its plebian nature. Haiku normally contain words suggesting a season, but most senryū have none. Haiku cover a variety of topics with (usually unspoken) parallels to human life, while the main concern of senryū is the manifold and often faintly absurd activities of people at every level of society. Both haiku and senryū are still very popular, and many newspapers and magazines have columns especially reserved for amateur poets. Although sometimes it is difficult to distinguish absolutely between haiku and senryū, we may say that one end of a continuous 5-7-5 poetic spectrum is colored by nature and the season, while at the other end, human figures are the direct focus. Haiku is an art of abbreviation and leaves space for the reader's imagination, while senryū tends to draw a scene succinctly and clearly. Let's examine some examples of haiku and senryū.

> The coat
> runs through the sudden rain
> without a head

In this senryū, the picture of the flustered man covering himself with his coat is as sharp as French artist Daumier's visual caricatures. Buson's haiku picture is quite different.

> Spring rain—
> telling stories as they go
> umbrella and raincoat

In both verses, we do not see people's faces. There is, however, a difference in the rain; one is a shower and the other is a spring drizzle. The senryū delineates a fleeting scene focusing on the running man, while haiku presents a world of watercolor painting where the soft enveloping rain is as important as the figures. Each reader can imagine the content of the people's conversation—are they mere acquaintances? Or are they lovers? Their talk blends softly into the rain. The reader of the senryū is a keen observer, while the reader of the haiku receives an invitation to participate in the scene.

Senryū runs a gamut of laughter from genteel to vulgar, and from good-natured to biting sarcasm, but the humor usually comes from the outside observation of human affairs. For example, merchants, driven by strict business ethics, usually all open their stores at the same time as the town starts its bustling day, but a poet observes an exception:

> On New Year's Day
> the morning in town
> comes irregularly

Senryū often depict human traits such as the eagerness of an avid player of *shōgi* (Japanese chess):

> The *shōgi* buff
> lines up the pieces
> even of his opponent

The poison of blowfish is well known. Even today some people die from the dish when it is prepared by an amateur. But, ah, the delicacy of it!

> "We die once anyway"
> and he eats
> the blowfish
> *Rakusai*

Senryū can be sarcastic. In Japan, babies are taught to clench their tiny fists, encouraged by "Oh, you do *nigi-nigi* (clenching) so well!" This innocent play becomes the source for a sly dig:

> The official's baby
> learns very well
> to grab with his hands

Alas, bribery is not unknown in any society.

Parody is a rich source for humor, and both haiku and senryū are sensitive to its delightful twists. Bashō, inarguably the most eminent haiku master, composed this haiku on snow in lighthearted vein:

> "Goodbye, goodbye"
> till I fall down—
> snow-viewing

This haiku becomes the source of a parody for a senryū:

> "Goodbye, goodbye"
> till I find—
> a pub

Bashō is best known for his verse on a frog:

> Old pond—
> a frog jumps in
> the sound of water

Bōsai, born about a hundred years later, comments:

> Old pond—
> after jumping in
> no more frog

There is still some respect for Bashō in Bōsai's parody, but another senryū by Kankan makes a wry comment:

> Master Bashō—
> at the sound of "splash!"
> he stops

If the master is looking for his second chance for fame, the great poet becomes the prey for senryū.

Since senryū depict situations clearly, they often come close to creating maxims. Hearing a senryū, the reader may laugh, saying, "This is so true!" or, "Yes, I've seen something similar!" Senryū's aphorism-like character, along with its 5-7-5 syllabic form, has become so ingrained in the mass mind that Japanese police today often issue signs for traffic control in this format to catch people's attention. Street signs and posters may carry:

> Don't rush out!
> cars cannot stop
> right away!

There are many similar signs about speeding, traffic lights, and so forth. A comedian then came up with a witty saying:

> The red traffic light—
> if we all cross together
> nothing to fear!

This poem became so well known that a recent newspaper used it for its headline when Japanese Diet members, who are very conscientious about wearing conservative attire, were encouraged to dress casual during the summer heat to conserve energy.

Neckties—
if we all take them off together
nothing to fear!

If senryū is an equalizer where any human could be a target of laughter, haiku is more of a harmonizer. In haiku, all creatures, including vegetation, become cohabitants of this world.

Planting my buttocks
on a huge taro leaf—
moon-viewing
Haritsu

Then, perhaps in a nearby vegetable field:

Very squarely
it sets its buttocks down—
the pumpkin
Sōseki

Both pairs of buttocks claim their unique and different existence, yet both are firmly set on the same earth.

The Woodblock Prints

There is a great deal of humor in much of Japanese art, and images in traditional woodblock prints are no exception. Even the most serious artists enjoyed a touch of the comic from time to time, as did the most serious haiku poets. This can be seen in single-sheet *ukiyo-e* prints, but even more fully in the form of woodblock books. Although these books were created by the same methods as the single-sheet prints, they are much less known, even though they were designed by artists of every school and tradition in Japan beginning in the seventeenth century. Instead of representing only the "floating world"—whose subjects included beautiful courtesans, actors, and travel landscapes—woodblock books show a wide world of subjects, including human figures of all kinds, other living creatures, and scenes of Japanese life.

In addition, as with senryū, a new style of purely humorous pictures became popular in the early eighteenth century. These were called *Toba-e* ("Toba-pictures") after Toba Sōjō, the purported painter of the "Animal Frolics" hand scroll of the twelfth century. Although some of the artists in this genre are known, they are largely anonymous, just like many senryū poets. Of all Japanese images, Toba-e are perhaps closest to our own humorous comic-book illustrations, with highly simplified figures displaying exaggerated limbs, over-the-top facial expressions, and a tremendous sense of energy. They ridicule everything from daily activities to traditional festivals, and from drunks to preachers to proper citizens, all without malice. The works in this book listed as "Anonymous" are all in the Toba-e tradition.

Humor also found an outlet in the works of more serious artists such as Yamaguchi Soken, who was most famous for his carefully painted portrayals of beautiful women. Yet in his book *Yamato jinbutsu gafu* (Pictures of Japanese People) of 1800, Soken created a number of designs that display his wry understanding of human foibles in the context of everyday life. Although his usual painting style was naturalistic, in these woodblock books Soken was able to capture a scene, an emotion, or a personality in a few brisk, succinct strokes of the brush. Even major Zen masters such as Hakuin and Sengai had their bold ink paintings recreated in woodblock books, including their versions of the comic.

Similarly, the early twentieth-century master Kamisaka Sekka had a sharp eye for potential sources of humor, although his artistic style was quite different from that of Soken. Sekka's book *Kokkei zuan* (Droll Pictures) of 1903 combines the powerfully simplified designs of the decorative *Rimpa* school of painting with his own personal taste for the absurd; the results are unexpected and delightful. The art of Sekka also comes close to abstraction at times, although one can often find a visual pun in his humorous works when one looks closely.

Our only exception to art from woodblock books comes in several selections included here from an album that was painted, rather than printed, by the late nineteenth-century artist Nakajima Yoshiume. He reveled in the strange, humorous, and grotesque in these small paintings, even more than in his single-sheet prints.

Clearly, humor in art did not depend upon the school or style of the painter. Even literati poet-painters, schooled in the Chinese tradition with its strong Confucian roots, allowed themselves to be playful in their designs for woodblock books, as can be seen in this volume. Poking fun was clearly something important to artists, as well as poets, of many kinds. As an invaluable element in many aspects of early modern Japanese culture, humor was not only a joy and pleasure, but it also served as a safety valve for people living highly restricted lives in a tightly bound society. What you cannot change, you may at least laugh at, and we hope that the poetry and art in this volume can still elicit smiles from our readers.

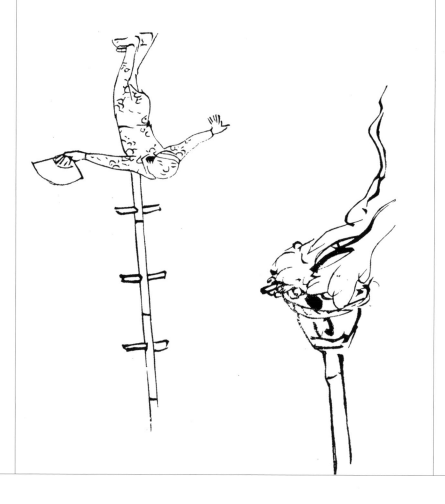

Human
Foibles

Feigning sleep—
the snoring is
too sincere

Anonymous

空寝入り
あまり鼾が
律儀過ぎ

Having given his opinion
he returns home to
his wife's opinion

Yachō

意見して
帰れば妻に
意見され
夜潮

Priding himself
on scolding
his beautiful wife

Anonymous

美しい
女房叱るが
自慢にて

Coming for a loan
he looks
especially honest

Anonymous

借りに
来た時は
正直そうな顔

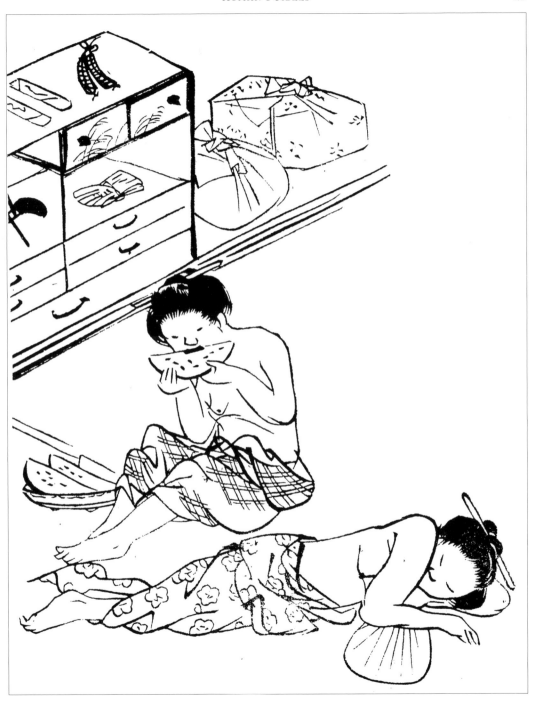

"Every woman"
he starts to say,
then looks around
Anonymous

すべて女
と言う者はと
そこらを見

As she talks
about her daughter-in-law
she mimics her
Anonymous

嫁のこと
姑身振り
して話し

"After you die
they'll be valuable"
he tells the painter
Anonymous

死ぬと値が
すると絵かきを
惨い評

Seductive words—
when she glances all around
it means she agrees

Anonymous

口説かれて
あたりを見るは
承知なり

Rather than money
he gives plenty
of advice

Anonymous

貸さぬくせ
意見がましい
ことを言い

Trying so hard
to be logical—
 the drunkard
  Meitei

筋道を
たてようとする
　酔っぱらい
　　迷亭

He saved tons
of money and died—
just asking them to fight
Hakuchō

争えと
いわんばかりに
ためて死に
白蝶

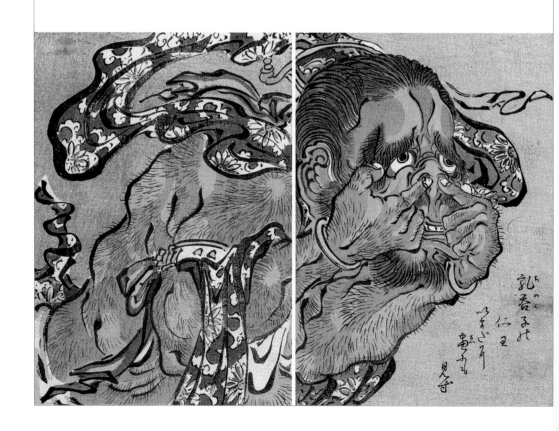

The foolish couple
mimicking the erotic picture
sprained their wrists
Anonymous

馬 鹿 夫 婦
春 画 を ま ね て
手 を く じ き

In humans
nothing is worse than
cleverness
Onitsura

人 間 の
知 恵 ほ ど
悪 い も の は な し
鬼 貫

The convalescent—
indulging in his mother's care
has become a habit
Anonymous

病 み 上 が り
母 を 遣 う が
く せ に な り

New Year's cards
with ladies' handwriting
get looked at first
Biriken

年賀状
女文字から
　先へ見る
　　美里劔

Two mistresses
beautiful
as knives
Anonymous

妾二人
刃物のように
美しき

She lowers
her eloquent lap
onto his silent lap
Anonymous

口利かぬ
膝へ口利く
膝をのせ

One umbrella—
the person more in love
gets wet

Keisanjin

もあいがさ
惚れてる方が
余計濡れ

慶山人

Catching up
and looking at her—
nothing special

Anonymous

追い付いて
見ればふだんの
女なり

Somehow unseemly
the man who fusses over his wife
too much
Anonymous

女房を
大切にする
見苦しさ

Not so popular
as to make his wife
worry
Anonymous

女房の
じれるほどには
持てぬなり

Whispering
and then laughing out loud—
how detestable!

Anonymous

低く言い
高く笑うは
　　にくらしい

Chanting the Lotus Sutra—
only his lips
are busy

Anonymous

法華経の
唇ばかり
　　いそがしき

Everyone unhappy
with their roles—
community theater
Anonymous

役不足
だらけ素人の
芝居なり

By saying not to worry
he says something
worrisome
Anonymous

気には
かけられなと
かけら事を言い

Stomping out angry—
the umbrella
opens too far
Anonymous

腹立って
出る傘は
開き過ぎ

"This won't hurt"
says the surgeon
taking out his scalpel
Anonymous

痛いこと
ないと外科どの
針を出し

Very secretly
the medicine peddler
    is sick
        Anonymous

極内で
かくらんをする
　　じょうさい売

Looking foolish
while waiting for
the next sneeze
Anonymous

後のくさめを
待っている
馬鹿なつら

Being called "Madame"
she paid
a few cents more
Anonymous

奥様と
言われて四五銭
高く買い

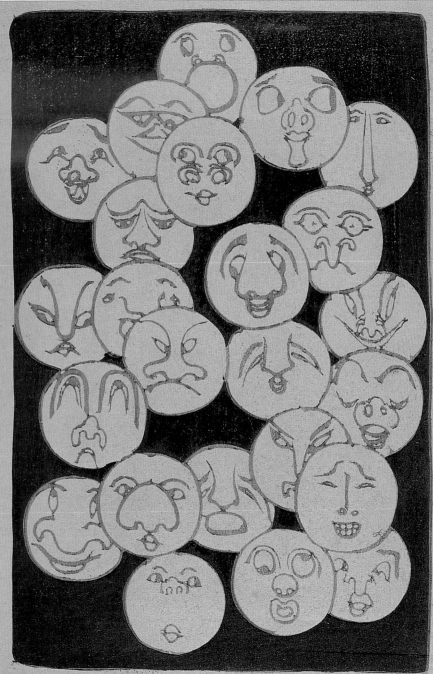

Losing
he straightens in his seat
and loses again
Itto

負けつづけ
すわり直して
又負ける
一斗

People fishing,
people watching people fishing,
people, people
Anonymous

釣る奴も
釣る奴見る
奴も奴

Taking a nap
looks more refined
   when holding a book
Anonymous

うたたねも
上品そうなのは
本を持ち

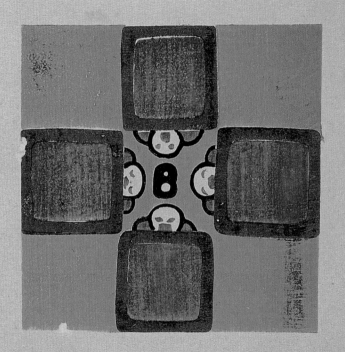

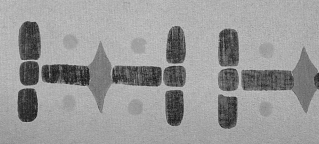

Totally flustered
he pretends to be calm and pulls out
his stethoscope

Ichiro

悠然と
実はあわてた
聴診器

伊知呂

At the ticket window
our child becomes
one year younger

Seiun

改札で
我が子の年
一つ減り

静雲

The mother
adds her support
to her son's lie

Anonymous

母親は
息子の嘘を
足してやり

Listening to his dad's advice

he has something else

in mind

Anonymous

意見聞く

息子の胸に

一物あり

What he had learned

was a nuisance

to his next teacher

Anonymous

習うたを

後の師匠に

邪魔がられ

"Let's pull them all"

says the dentist

generously

Anonymous

皆ぬいて

しまえと歯医者

惜気なし

While he yawns widely
his hand stretches
toward the food
Kakō

食 い 物 の
方 へ 手 が 出 る
大 欠 伸
可 香

"In wrestling
I would never have lost"—
pillow talk
Buson

負 ま じ き
角 力 を 寝 も の
が た り 哉
蕪 村

Having children,
you understand—
but too late
Anonymous

子を持って
知るとはおそい
思いつき

The Human
Touch

Spring rain
I gave my yawn
   to the dog at the gate
      Issa

春雨や
欠伸をうつる
  門の犬
    一茶

Sharing the same blood
but we're not related—
   the hateful mosquito!
      Jōsō

血を分けし
身とは思はず
  蚊の憎さ
    丈草

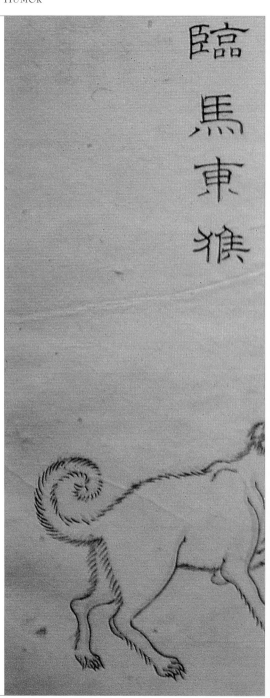

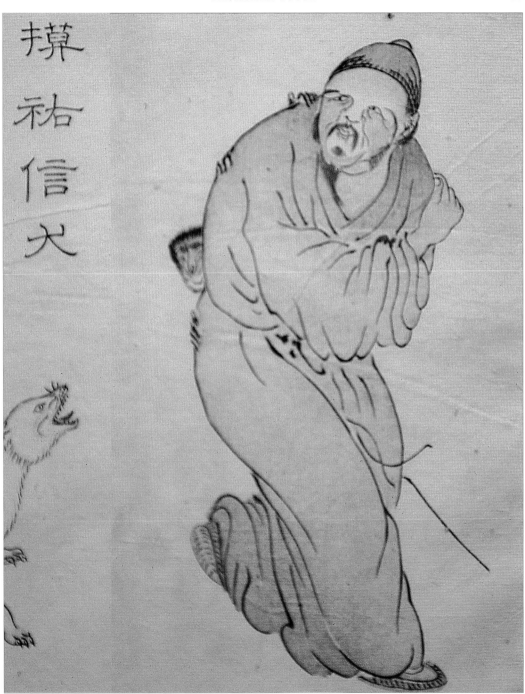

I will sweep you

to your partner—

the cricket

Jōsō

つれのある

所へ掃くぞ

きりぎりす

丈草

Swatting a fly
I chant a sutra
"Namu Amida Buddha"

Issa

蠅一つ
打っては
なむあみだ仏哉
一茶

Trying not to disturb
the snow on my hat—
I take it off and look

Anonymous

笠の雪
崩れぬように
脱いで見

Morning glories—
even from unskilled brushes
they look elegant

Bashō

朝顔は
下手のかくさへ
哀なり
芭蕉

The sumo wrestler—
just around his breasts
a crowd gathers
Anonymous

関取の
乳のあたりに
人だかり

My *go* rival—
how vexing
and how dear
Anonymous

碁 敵 は

憎 さ も 憎 し

な つ か し き

Unaware
of a thief's gaze—
chilled melons

Issa

盗人の
見るともしらぬ
冷やし瓜
　一茶

A bachelor
does not feel like groaning
even when sick
Kinbō

ひとり者
病気も唸る
気になれず
きん坊

Even the winner
of the argument
has a hard time sleeping
Gyokutorō

言い勝った
方もその夜を
寝そびれる
玉兎朗

After my sneeze
all is quiet—
summer mountains
Yasui

くっさめの
跡しづか也
なつの山
野水

Trout fishing—
more fishermen
than trout
Kenjin

鮎 を 釣 る
人 が 鮎 よ り
多 い な り
剣 人

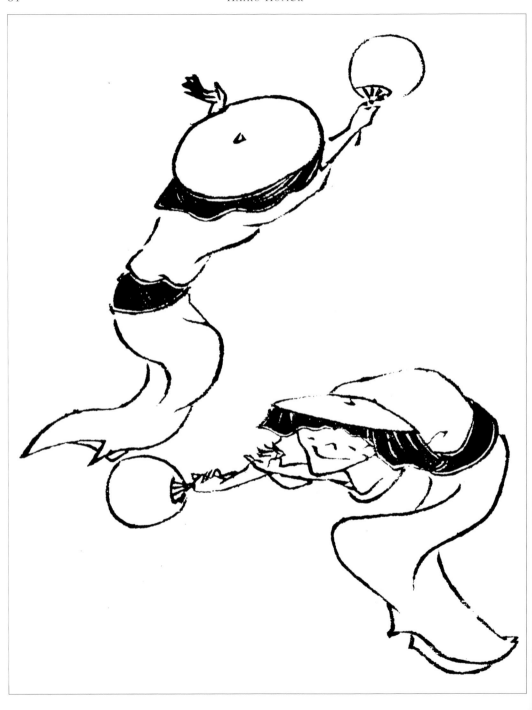

The chestnut
I cannot reach—
how large, how splendid!
Issa

ひろわれぬ
栗の見事よ
大きさよ
一茶

Planting my buttocks
on a huge taro leaf—
moon-viewing
Haritsu

芋の葉に
尻をすえたる
月見かな
把栗

At the sound of footsteps
it divided in two—
the shadow
Anonymous

足音で
二つに割れる
影法師

The coat
runs through the sudden rain
without a head
Anonymous

首のない
羽織が走る
俄雨

Entering the ring
none of the wrestlers
looks like a loser
Anonymous

土俵入り
負ける景色は
見えぬなり

At the auction
even Amida Buddha
is evaluated
Ryūkō

競売に
阿弥陀如来も
見積もられ
流虹

Answering
from the dentist's chair
"uh . . . uh . . . uh . . ."
        Bunzō

歯 科 患 者
アーアーアーで
　答えをし
　　文 象

With both hands
thrust up mightily—
   my yawn
     Anonymous

両の手で
あくびをぐっと
   さしあげる

While he's dozing
the wind is turning
   the pages of his book
     Anonymous

うたた寝の
書物は
   風がくっている

"Bring your bowl and chopsticks!"
I bang on
  my neighbor's wall

Anonymous

わんとはし
持って来やれと
壁をぶち

I pull my neck
deep into the muffler—
winter moon

Sanpū

襟巻きに
首引きいれて
冬の月
　　杉風

My nose running
I play a solitary *go*-game
night chill

Buson

洟たれて
独り碁をうつ
夜寒かな
　　蕪村

Craning my neck
to watch myself lying down—
Oh, it's cold

Raizan

我が寝たを
首あげて見る
寒さかな
　　来山

"Don't dare break it!"
but he broke off and gave me
a branch of garden plum

Taigi

な折りそと
折りてくれけり
園の梅
太祇

Taking a nap—
the roof over his face
made by a book

Anonymous

うたた寝の
顔へ一冊
屋根をふき

The flute player
bitten by a mosquito
on the edge of his lips
Kyoriku

笛吹きの

蚊にくはれけり

口の端

許六

Here we are
all skeletons—
evening cool

Issa

こう居るも
皆がい骨ぞ
夕涼み

一茶

Autumn passing—
I hug my knees
so close to me

Taigi

行秋や
抱けば身に添ふ
膝頭

太祇

Truly the autumn has come—
I was convinced
by my sneeze

Buson

秋来ぬと
合点させたる
くさめかな

蕪村

Visitors
kindly create a path
through the snow at my gate

Issa

来る人が
道つける也
門の雪

一茶

I poked the snow
with a yardstick
for my diary

Anonymous

物差しで
雪をつっ突く
日記づけ

Cats eyes
children's hearts
autumn sky—all fickle
Anonymous

猫 の 目 と
子 供 心 や
秋 の 空

Walking the dog
you meet
lots of dogs
Sōshi

犬 つ れ て
歩 け ば 犬 に
よ く 出 会 い
操 子

One sneeze—
and I lost sight of
the skylark
Yayū

く さ め し て
見 失 い た る
雲 雀 か な
也 有

Scorned by
fleas and flies
another day ends
     Issa

蚤 蠅 に
あ な ど ら れ つ つ
け ふ も 暮 れ ぬ
     一 茶

A New Year's card
to my cat
from its vet
      Yorie

ね こ に 来 る
賀 状 や 猫 の
く す し よ り
     よ り 江

That snowman looks
just like someone—
I glance and pass by

Gessō

たれやらに
似し雪だるま
見て過ぎる
月草

Secret rendezvous at night—
a mosquito was swatted
and died quietly

Anonymous

忍ぶ夜の
蚊はたたかれて
そっと死に

One person
and also one fly
in the great hall

Issa

人一人
蠅も一つや
大座敷
一茶

SMILES WITH NATURE

From the nose
of the Buddha in the fields—
icicles

Issa

野仏の
鼻の先から
氷柱かな
　　一茶

Hearing one jump
they all jump—
frogs

Wakyū

一つ飛ぶ
音に皆飛ぶ
蛙かな
　　和及

The fly on the porch
while rubbing its hands—
swat!

Issa

縁 の 蝿
手 を 擦 る と こ ろ を
打 た れ け り
一 茶

A bat
hanging from the arm of
the temple guardian god

Issa

こ う も り や
仁 王 の 腕 に
ぶ ら さ が る
一 茶

The bird set free—
so happy
it bumps into a tree

Anonymous

う れ し さ の
木 に つ き あ た る
放 し 鳥

During the day
the Buddha shelters behind
mosquitoes

Issa

昼 の 蚊 を
後 ろ に か く す
仏 か な

一 茶

Pursued,
it hides in the moon—
the firefly

Ryōta

追 わ れ て は
月 に 隠 る る
蛍 か な

良 太

Opening the red gate
of the Ant King's Palace—
a peony

Buson

蟻 王 宮
朱 門 を 開 く
ぼ た ん か な

蕪 村

The autumn mosquito
ready for death
stings me
Shiki

秋 の 蚊 や
死 ぬ る 覚 悟 で
我 を さ す
子 規

As flies retreat
mosquitoes start
their battle cry
Anonymous

蠅 が 陣 を
引 き 蚊 が
と き の 声

The bat's
secret home—
a tattered hat
Buson

こ う も り の
か く れ 住 み け り
破 れ 笠
蕪 村

Tame ducks
stretch their necks
hoping to see the world
Kōji

家鴨首
のばして世間
見るつもり
光路

Dashing into one another

whispering, parting—

ants

Anonymous

突 き あ た り

何 か 囁 き

蟻 わ か れ

Frogs grow silent—

noble humans

are passing by

Rakukyo

蛙 黙 す

人 間 様 の

お 通 り

楽 居

The black dog
becomes a lantern—
snowy road
Anonymous

黒犬を
提灯にする
雪の道

Its face
looks like a horse—
the grasshopper
Anonymous

面さしは
馬に似ている
きりぎりす

Each tree
announces its name
at sprouting time
Issa

木々おのおの
名乗り出てたる
木の芽哉
一茶

On my shoulder
is it longing for a companion?
a red dragonfly

Sōseki

肩に来て

人懐かしや

赤蜻蛉

漱石

The moon in the water
turning somersaults
flows away

Ryōta

水の月
もんどりうって
流れけり

良太

Making fun
of a floating shoe—
plovers

Anonymous

浮沓を
馬鹿にしている
都鳥

Urging me to steal
just this branch of plum blossoms—
the moon

Issa

梅の花を
ここを盗めと
さす月か

一茶

Nonchalantly
standing in the harvest moonlight—
the scarecrow

Issa

名月に
けろりと立ちし
かかしかな
　　一茶

Embarrassed
when its hat falls off—
the scarecrow

Buson

笠とれて
面目もなき
かかしかな
　　蕪村

The man raking
keeps being called back
by the leaves

Anonymous

掃 除 す る
人 を 木 の 葉 が
呼 び 戻 す

Looking as though
he owns the Imperial lodging—
a snail

Issa

御 旅 所 を
吾 も の 顔 や
蝸 牛

一 茶

As the lake breeze
cools his ass
  the cicada cries
     Issa

湖 に
尻 を 吹 か せ て
  蝉 の な く
    一 茶

As lightning flashes
he strokes his head—
the toad

Issa

稲妻に
つむりなでけり
引蟇

一茶

Turning into a Buddha
in the autumn dusk—
the badger

Buson

秋のくれ
仏に化ける
狸かな
蕪村

In the shimmering haze
the cat mumbles something
in its sleep

Issa

陽炎に
何やら猫の
寝言かな
一茶

The bitter persimmons
spending their autumn
quietly

Rito

しぶ柿の
閑かに秋を
送りけり
吏登

The praying mantis
angry as it tumbles
is swept away
Ōjō

蟷螂の
怒りまろびて
掃かれけり
王城

Overflowing with love
the cat as coquettish
as a courtesan
Saimaro

愛あまる
猫は傾婦の
媚をかる
才麿

Both partners
sport whiskers—
cats' love

Raizan

両 方 に
髭 が あ る な り
猫 の 恋

来 山

Day slowly ending—
its tummy on the ground
the dog stretches

Shōzan

遅 き 日 や
土 に 腹 つ く
犬 の 伸 び

嘯 山

Cats' love—
they parted
without ceremony
        Issa

猫 の 恋
打 切 棒 に
分 か れ け り
        一 茶

Being hit
the gong spits out
a noon-time mosquito
        Sōseki

叩 か れ て
昼 の 蚊 を 吐 く
木 魚 か な
        漱 石

Just like people
the monkey clasps its hands—
autumn wind
        Shadō

人 に 似 て
猿 も 手 を く む
秋 の 風
        酒 堂

When I show my delight
they fall down faster—
acorns

Fūsei

喜べば
しきりに落つる
木の実かな
風生

From the sleeve
of a scarecrow
the bright moon
Issa

名月や
山のかがしの
袂から
一茶

The saddle taken off
how cold it looks—
the horse's rump
Hekigodō

鞍とれば
寒き姿や
馬の尻
碧梧桐

It intends to present
some argument—
   the frog

Issa

一理屈
いう気で居る
  蛙かな

一茶

Very squarely
it sets its buttocks down—
   the pumpkin

Sōseki

どっしりと
尻を据えたる
  南瓜かな

漱石

THE ARTISTS

Hakuin Ekaku (1685–1768) The most important Zen master of the past five hundred years, Hakuin used many methods of reaching people, including public Zen meetings as well as painting, calligraphy, and poetry. His use of humor was a major feature of his work.

Kamisaka Sekka (1866–1942) Recently becoming better known in both Japan and the West, Sekka was one of the great artist-designers of the twentieth century, adding new interpretations to the Rimpa (decorative) tradition. His woodblock book prints are especially fine, and often show his original sense of humor.

Kawamura Bumpō (1779–1821) A successful Kyoto painter in the *Kishi* (naturalistic) tradition, Bumpō became especially celebrated for his woodblock books, which he created in both Japanese and Chinese styles.

Kawanabe Kyōsai (Gyōsai, 1831–1889) Although Kyōsai was trained as a painter in the academic Kanō School, his independent and often wildly imaginative spirit led him to become well known, sometimes notorious, as a print-designer, painter, and lover of wine.

Ki Baitei (1744–1810) A pupil of the haiku poet and painter Yosa Buson, Baitei lived in Shiga, outside Kyoto, and excelled in landscape and figure paintings and prints.

Kitao Masatoshi (1764–1824) Known for his work in the field of popular prints as Kitao Masayoshi, he later studied in the official Kanō School and took the name Kuwagata Keisai.

Kobayashi Kiyochika (1847–1915) Noted as an ukiyo-e painter and print designer, Kiyochika included some Western artistic techniques in many of his prints.

Matsuya Jichōsai (flourished 1781–1788) Also known as Nichōsai, he was a sake brewer and antique dealer in Osaka who dabbled in poetry, painting, and singing. His humorous paintings have a caricature style all their own.

Miyamoto Kunzan (dates unknown) A literati painter who lived in Osaka, Kunzan is little known today, but worked in the Chinese scholar-artist tradition.

Nakajima Yoshiume (1819–1879) A student of Kunisada, Yoshiume lived most of his life in Osaka where he became know for his woodblock prints as well as book illustrations.

Niwa Kagen (1742–1786) A painter from Nagoya, Kagen was one of the first artists in the literati (*Nanga*) school in his area.

Sakai Hōitsu (1761–1828) The second son of a feudal lord, Hōitsu became a Buddhist priest to avoid family duties, and then settled in Edo (Tokyo) to live an artistic life that included creating paintings, woodblock prints, and haiku.

Santō Kyōden (1761–1816) A leading writer of popular fiction, Kyōden used the name Kitao Masanobu as an artist.

Sengai Gibon (1750–1837) A Zen master from Kyushu, Sengai became beloved for his paintings, which often show his delightful sense of humor.

Suzuki Fuyō (1749–1816) A poet-artist in Edo (Tokyo), Fuyō worked in the Chinese literati tradition.

Takehara Shunshōsai (active late eighteenth century) Working in the late eighteenth century, Shunshōsai designed many humorous pictures for woodblock books.

Tsuda Seifū (1880–1978) First studying Japanese-style painting, Seifū then went to Paris in 1907 to study oil painting; he eventually became highly successful in both styles.

Watanabe Kazan (1793–1841) A literati painter and patriot, Kazan worked in many styles including Chinese-style landscapes and Western-influenced portraiture. Before he was forced to commit suicide by the Shogunate, he also published a book of delightful *haiga* (haiku paintings).

Yamaguchi Soken (1759–1818) A pupil of the naturalistic master Maruyama Ōkyo, Soken became known for his paintings of Osaka beauties in a refined painting style, but he also produced woodblock books of Japanese figures and scenes.

THE POETS

Bashō (1644–1694) Widely admired as the greatest of all haiku masters, Bashō left samurai life when his lord passed away, and devoted himself to poetry. He made several journeys, which appeared in travelogues with prose and haiku. His deep sense of humanity and intense observation of the natural and human world combined to elevate the haiku tradition to its epitome.

Biriken (dates unknown)

Bunzō See Sekiguchi Bunzō

Buson See Yosa Buson

Fukuda Haritsu (1865–1944) Born in Shingū in Wakayama Prefecture, Haritsu became a pupil of Masaoka Shiki in Tokyo. He moved to Kyoto and led the life of a scholar-poet under the name of Kodōjin. He wrote haiku, *waka,* and Chinese-style poetry and painted both *haiga* (painting with haiku) and literati landscapes.

Fūsei See Tomiyasu Fūsei

Gessō See Itō Gessō

Gyokutorō See Takashima Gyokutorō

Hakuchō (dates unknown)

Haritsu See Fukuda Haritsu

Hekigodō See Kawahigashi Hekigodō

Ichiro See Kawamura Ichiro

Issa (1762–1826) A poet whose life was filled with personal tragedy, Issa wrote poems with such compassion for all living creatures that he became, with Bashō and Buson, one of the most loved poets in the haiku tradition.

Itō Gessō (1899–1946) A poet born in Nagano Prefecture, Gessō favored traditional style haiku over verses with less subtlety. He also did theoretical writing on haiku.

Itto See Yoshida Itto

Jōsō (1662–1704) Because of poor health, Jōsō gave up his life as a samurai at the age of twenty-six and became a monk. He studied haiku with Bashō, and after the death of his master, Jōsō lived a solitary life. He is regarded as one of Bashō's Ten Disciples.

Kakō (dates unknown)

Kawahigashi Hekigodō (1873–1937) Born in Matsuyama, Aichi Prefecture, Hekigodō studied with Shiki. He also wrote novels and literary criticism.

Kawamura Ichiro (1906–1963) Born in Osaka, Ichiro practiced medicine. He also wrote many essays.

Keisanjin (dates unknown)

Kenjin (dates unknown)

Kinbō See Yano Kinbō

Kōji (dates unknown)

Kubo Yorie (1884–1967) Born in Matsuyama, Yorie met Shiki and Sōseki when she was young and became interested in haiku.

Kyoriku (1656–1715) A samurai in the Hikone region, present-day Shiga Prefecture, Kyoriku excelled in the lance, sword, and horseback-riding. He was also a good painter in the Kanō style, and studied haiku with Bashō.

Masaoka Shiki (1867–1902) Despite the brevity of his life, Shiki became the most influential haiku poet and theorist of the late nineteenth century. He insisted that haiku poets should cultivate the keen observation (*shasei*) of nature. He established the famous haiku journal *Hototogisu*.

Meitei See Tsukakoshi Meitei

Natsume Sōseki (1867–1916) The most famous novelist of his time, Sōseki studied in England and later taught English literature in Japan. He wrote many fine haiku verses and Chinese-style poetry.

Ōjō See Tanaka Ōjō

Okada Yachō (1882–1960) Born in Tsuyama City, Yachō started composing senryū in his early twenties. He engaged in farming and was a gentle person known for senryū with topics taken from his daily life.

Onitsura (1661–1738) Onitsura gained recognition as a gifted haiku poet in his teens. He proclaimed that the important virtue of haiku is sincerity. He avoided being a professional poet and did not take in any pupils.

Raizan (1654–1716) A merchant in Osaka. He started with comical and witty haiku but later changed to a more serious style close to Bashō's.

Rakukyo (dates unknown)

Rito (1681–1755) An Edo poet, Rito was one of the pupils of Ransetsu, a leading poet of the time. Because of his illness, he led a quiet life away from the social world. Before he died, Rito ordered his pupils to burn all of his haiku except eighteen, but after his death, his followers edited and published his poems.

Ryōta See Sano Ryōta

Ryūkō (dates unknown)

Saimaro (1656–1738) Born to a samurai family, Saimaro studied haiku with Ihara Saikaku, the famous fiction writer and haiku poet of the time. Saimaro also kept an association with Bashō and had considerable power in the Osaka-area haiku circle.

Sanpū (1647–1732) Bashō's pupil and also his patron, Sanpū provided Bashō with his famous cottage Bashō-an (Banana-Plant Hermitage).

Sano Ryōta (1890–1954) Born in Nīgata Prefecture, Ryōta was known for his forceful haiku.

Seiun (dates unknown)

Sekiguchi Bunzō (1870–1962) Born in Tokyo, Bunzō was a high school teacher. He was influential in establishing ties among early modern senryū poets.

Shadō (d. 1737) A poet in the Bashō school, Shadō practiced medicine. He was known for his boisterous actions among his coterie.

Shiki See Masaoka Shiki

Shōzan (1718–1801) A poet in Kyoto, also known as Rittei. Besides haiku, he also composed Chinese-style poetry.

Sōseki See Natsume Sōseki

Sōshi (dates unknown)

Taigi (1709–1771) Born in Edo, Taigi moved to the entertainment district of Kyoto, where he became associated with Buson.

Takashima Gyokutorō (1887–1953) Born in Tokyo, Gyokutorō became a firefighter. He was influential among the senryū circle in Tokyo.

Tanaka Ōjō (1885–1939) A poet born in Kyoto, Ōjō became acquainted with Shiki when he was in his teens. He studied with the influential haiku poet Takahama Kyoshi.

Tomiyasu Fūsei (1885–1979) Fūsei traveled in Europe and the United States, then returned to Japan to study under

Takahama Kyoshi, a famous poet of the time. Eventually he became one of the leading haiku poets of the early twentieth century.

Tsukakoshi Meitei (1894–1965) A poet born in Tokyo, Meitei worked for newspaper companies, one of which was in Taiwan. He created a Taiwan senryū circle before returning to Japan after World War II.

Wakyū (dates unkown)

Yachō See Okada Yachō

Yano Kinbō (1889–1936) Born in Ibaragi Prefecture, Kinbō was also known as Kinrō. His father was a haiku poet. Kinbō created a senryū circle from which many poets emerged. He worked at a newspaper company, and later published popular writings on finance.

Yasui (1658–1743) A merchant from Nagoya, Yasui wrote many haiku following the Bashō tradition. Later in his life, Yasui shifted his interest to waka and the tea ceremony.

Yayū (1702–1783) A retainer of the Owari clan. After he retired, Yayū spent his life in creating haiku and paintings. Yayū was also known for his *haibun* (poetic writing).

Yorie See Kubo Yorie

Yosa Buson (1716–1783) In his teens, Buson went to Edo and studied painting and haiku, and later settled in Kyoto. Known as a celebrated haiku poet, Buson is also considered one of the greatest artists in the literati style of painting.

Yoshida Itto (1891–1961) A senryū poet born in Tokyo, Itto associated with many literary figures of the time. He is known for his sarcastic style.

THE ILLUSTRATIONS